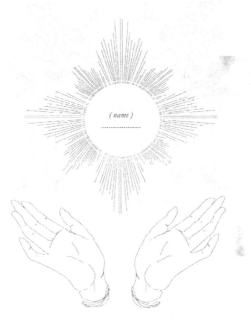

(name)
....

SELF–HEALER

Illustrations by Sez Kristiansen

Books can be made available for quantity discounts in
bulk purchases for educational, business or sales
promotional uses.

sezkristiansen.com
@sezkristiansen

Information and requests:
hello@sezkristiansen.com

May this book fall with divine timing to all those
brave souls who seek to find their wholeness in a
world of separation.

May we meet one day and give each other's
shadows thanks for the contrast they so
beautifully painted our lives with.

*This book is dedicated to my little world of blossoming humans.
Mads, Mathias & Siska.*

CONTENTS

INTRODUCTION

Intention
/ɪnˈtɛnʃ(ə)n/
A natural process of healing.

Y ou do not need to know *how* to heal yourself – just have the sincere desire to do so. This is the first and foremost step to which all holistic wellness flows forth. There is a grace that comes to those who recognize their intuitive need to hold space for healing because it is with this soul-nourishing intention that the universe will guide you to your own restorative super power of self-love. The universe has no greater wish than to be bound by the collective consciousness of love, for it heals a world that has spent too long in its paradox.

This little book of prose and poetry was created with the intention to permeate the instinctual feminine psyche into all perspectives of your healing. HER is the ultimate healer – she is the balancing, feminine weight on the spiritual scale that creates harmony in your physical life. She is within us all and unlike her male counterpart, holds immeasurable strength *because* of her sensitivity.

She is not like always made of light however, and is often found in the profound expression of darkness. She creates peaty, blackened soils to plant you in because she knows that your growth depends on the richness of your own experience.

HER needs are simple; to show you the way back to *wholeness* - but only once you have rested in the value of its contrast. When you embrace this allowing and expansive part of yourself into your pain, you will have the influence to heal generations' worth of wounds, which lie embedded in your psyche.

Your thoughts, emotions, and physical world create imbalances, to which you suffer most when you slip away from your intentions, stray from your core being, or more heinous - tell yourself untruths about who you are.

When fully re-calibrated within yourself, you are able to heal by honoring your emotions rather than excusing them. So listen to the subtle (and often inescapable) signs that you are being called into a state of healing. HER voice often calls by breaking down the body before the mind even becomes aware of HER presence. Your emotions can corrode, or they can create. It is up to you, everyday, which emotions you use to free yourself with.

HER space is always held for you when you decide that your pain no longer serves you. HER energy offers you the white oak taproots of inner grounding, so deeply implanted that you may spring as an offshoot from her stability – and she offers the compassion of intrinsic understanding, allowing you to reemerge back into your soul-life without judgment for your absence.

I am honored by the path you have decided to take to heal yourself, for your faith in self-restoration holds space for others too. It is, in fact, a selfless act to heal oneself and those who choose to come back into alignment are those who hold a healing space for others too. Sisters are bound together by their self-regeneration efforts and have a certain omnipotent power that raise those around them too. So be determined in your ability to heal by the quiet wrath of a collective consciousness – for we may start to heal the world itself.

You do not have to rise to meet yourself; it is never an *action* that needs to be taken in order to be who you truly are. Instead, it's a *letting go* that is imperative to healing. You can untether yourself from the expectation that you are to be happy all the time by simply honoring your own emotions and granting them space to show you what is out of alignment.

To be healed by HER feels like putting on your soul-skin again as she allows you to be creative, spontaneous and inspired by all that makes you truly authentic. HER energy allows you to connect - without resistance - to that empowered and passionate being that burns within you and that enkindles your creative forces.

Intentionally coming back into alignment feels like this fullness of possibility, this exciting and yet familiar wholeness. It feels like coming home, like ease, like confidence, like certainty, like freedom, and like the biggest love affair you've ever had with yourself. When you are in this state of oneness with your feminine consciousness and your physical body, you are fully immersed in the harmony of life because you are living in a way that is deeply nourishing to every aspect of both your spirituality and your humanity.

Healing is an individual quest, a solo journey, and a lonely emergence. It requires that you simply know that it's ok to feel good again. This low, this wound, this hurt, this hollowing, and this weight – it is not yours. It is simply a reminder that you need rest, to learn, to gather strength so that you may continue after a period of convalescence. The pain was never meant to stay, to bunk-up with you forever, to keep poking at you whenever you dare smile. It was made to remind you that nothing in life is solid and nor should you try holding on to the things that make you feel certain - for even your wounds can become your absolute when you keep them festered.

If you have the desire to live fully right now, you have the chance to experience all life's crests and nadirs without letting them anchor or overthrow you. This innate need to heal yourself is intuitive guidance back to your True North and your fully aligned Self again.

May your body rest deeply, your soul alight unashamedly and your heart beat brazenly. May your vibration rise so high that you brush the soft heels of the universe as she dances in honor.

Welcome dear One, with the infallible HER within, let us journey with an intention to heal - inwards and upwards.

WAKE UP, WAKE UP, WAKE UP.
Do you remember this place,
of sun's eclipse
from where you came?

Where you rested for eons
in the deep sleep
of the innocent.

Do you remember
when spiral nebulas and star clusters
woke you from your slumber
with stardust kisses
and pearly caresses,
gifting you with the residue
of Mother Devi's love.

You still have the *umbra* soul
and fidelity to source -
and when you lose your luminesce
there is always a way back to HER,
for she waits
ever-patiently
for you to return home.

Wake up, wake up, wake up
and remember from where you came.

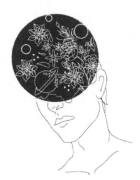

MAY THE VIOLET LIGHT
of our wounds
show others the way.

We are the scar-squad
of tattooed priestesses,
of soul sorceresses,
and may all those
who feel that their imperfections
are what makes them
incandescent
join our survival of the sacred.

We are not
frayed thread,
caught in stormy sky,
but star-shard,
cut from the universe herself.

RISE WITH ME
oh, shackled one, with
heels still pinned to floor.

I will help you lift your
bones, so that you can
feel the lightness of your soles
as they touch
the very ashes that still smolder
from where you burned.

Rise with me,
for I am your cinder sister,
your kindle-creator,
and reminder of your renewal.

Let me torch your wings once again,
for there is much work
to do with the ash remains.

WHAT IS THE SONG
from your soul
that eludes you?
The heart's harp
that untethers you?

Your soul is a siren
and calls to you from its depths.

And just like the mythological creature,
you too will perish if you hear HER song
and escape without answering.

Listen, oh listen with attention and courage.

Do not turn away.
Do not fear your calling…

But listen and lose yourself fully
to the melody of Spirit.

FIND THE WOUND.
Find the word
that describes the wound.

Know the wound.
Honor the emotion
that encompasses the wound.

Cleanse the wound.
Awaken the light
that acknowledges the wound.

Heal the wound.
Allow the action
that absolves the wound.

- A mantra

THERE IS NO LOVE LOSS
like the one
that destroys
yourself.

For what a stranger
can split in two,
you can sever
from source.

And what a lover
can break in half,
you can shatter
into oblivion.

There is no love gained
like the one
cultivated within yourself.

For what another
can give you in moment,
you can keep for yourself
eternally.

SOMETIMES,
the midday's moon
will slip through
the tracing paper sky
and remind me
that the sun is
but a momentary eclipse
to what is
the vast darkness
of the universe.

And my true nature
is not held
within these twelve hours
of shadow makings,
but freed
when the raven black sky
comes to take me home.

SACRED ARE THE LONELY ARMS
that make you realize
your love was worth more substance.

Be grateful to those empty places,
those shallow'd beings,
who talk about depth
without ever having dug at
their own core.

For they are our reminders
of the fickle surface dwellers,
who are yet to know the markings
of the smoldering magma soul.

And this, to one of substance,
is rarer than the saffron
that lingerers upon the crocus
in spring's final thaw.

ALIGNMENT

Living in alignment with your true nature, with an intention to persistently heal throughout your life, is no a means for a cure. We are all, *in life-terms*, incurable. Death *is* the only cure, and it always comes too early for us to be able to gain valuable hindsight.

So better plead insanity now and live in the liberation of lunacy. For, to lose one's mind is a sure way to adapt to the ultimatum that life is liquid and volatile.

In a state of flow, we are able rise and fall, neither playing too long in the shallows nor resting too deep in the ocean's indigos. Our strength lies in our ability to surface without the Benz and without the desperacy to free dive back – deeper – just so that we may feel the compounding silence again.

Acknowledging that you are in need of healing is your rebirth into a quicksilver life.

YOUR HEART WAS MADE
for holes,
for indents,
nicks and notches.

It is made porous
with every hurt.

It is made permeable
with every hit.

And so
your love
becomes your own oasis
in life's drought and scarcity.

MY VOICE
became a tool
and lost its silence.

My body
became a conduit of self-love
and lost its abuse.

My mind
became still
and lost its dominance.

My heart
became a home
and lost its longing.

This is how we live, awake.

WHAT THE HEART FEELS,
the mind sees,
the tongue cuts
the hands shape
the eyes store
and the belly holds.

So cleanse the pain
and raise your emotions
to those which feel good,
feel full,
feel whole,
feel true,
and all will be created
in the honor of love…

For there is no greater maker.

THE MOST SACRED OF TOOLS
known to woman
is her ability to mold,
to knead,
to peel off
and to flesh out
all that keeps her life
enclosed in the glass cabinet.

Saving her best
for service and Sundays,
for tomorrows and one days,
for laters and maybes,
for after-motherhoods
but before-end days.

Women were made to live
by their own passion-driven hands
and in that primal creation,
hold palms up
and knuckles down
for our foremothers past
who were unable
to heal themselves.

Their hands were
unwittingly shackled
and bereft of care,
or worse,
free but unscathed
by life's cuts and grazes
that make for strong grips
and robust self-mendings.

To begin to heal is to plant, deep
into nourished earth, a future
to which all daughters
carry the inheritance
of the silver scalloped bones
of self-creation.
Which engraved, like moon markings,
hold the verse:

"I sway to the rhythm,
my palms on this waste,
hand-creation to birth-creation,
I move at my own pace"

LISTEN, LEARN OR LET GO.
This is what I choose to ask
whenever I am met by the
resistance of life.

Listen, learn or let go?

- A Mantra

I WAITED
for him
to understand
what I felt.

I waited
for him
to see
what only I could.

But the longer I waited,
the more I lost myself
in the need for permission.

So instead of waiting,
I started inspiring.

I gave myself
the permission
to be
who *I* wanted
to be,
and realized
I could validate
myself.

And so I stepped
into my own truth,
one breathe
one beat
one foot at a time.

And with that confidence
and conviction,
I no longer needed him
to see me.

And all of a sudden, he saw everything.

THE WAY OF THE SACRED FEMININE
is about joining things
that were never meant
to be apart.

The mind, the body,
power and vulnerability,
the determined foot
and the loving heart.

DO NOT LET YOUR UNIQUENESS
carve sharp corners
where soft curves
used to be.

Let it enforce
the love
you have
for those few
who share
your vision.

Not validate your
beliefs of separateness.

WHEN YOU LONG FOR SOMETHING,
make sure your desire of it burns
greater than your fear of it.

For faith in passion
has the power
to turn trauma
into healing,
struggle
into growth,
and despair
into desire.

And so shall fear become
but a dewdrop to a furnace.

WE MAY NEVER TRULY HEAL
by turning our backs to the future,
for the shadows of the past
will surely engulf us,
and like quicksand,
bury us in the density
of our own grief.

We may, however,
always be nourished
by the *now* and the *future*,
for both hold open spaces
for change,
and therefore
immeasurable possibility:
an uncharted certitude
for all who dare to look for potential.

YOU CAN BARRICADE YOUR HEART.
Make pitchforks out of arteries,
moats out of veins
and drawbridges out of valves,
but your heart is still just a muscle
and it can only ever strengthen itself
through the wars of love.

BE UNCONVENTIONAL IN EVERYTHING
you do.

Unconventional in how you see yourself.
Unconventional in what you wear.
Unconventional in how you work.
Unconventional in how you live, speak & act.

Begin to see that everything has an
unconventional potential.
   Begin   to see that
EVERYTHING unconventional is in   fact
the *real* YOU,
and that by   reaching
       beyond   what is considered N O R
M A L, you start   to see yourself
       as **you** really   ARE
& suddenly you begin to feel   more and
MORE   *(- inexplicably -)*
             F R E E.

And that perhaps you will unexpectedly walk your
own unconventional path right out of your
conventional life - and into one that leads you to
all kinds of exciting ideas and experiences.

And perhaps one day, one of those ideas will just happen to change the world. After all, no ordinary idea has ever made an extraordinary change. It takes the weird, the outcast, the fringe-dwellers, the medial, the radical, the misfit and the intuitive to create a world worth living in.

So whatever you do, don't be normal. We have too many of those already.

WOMAN IS SPLIT IN TWO.
The mirror in her
was made
so that one hand,
one foot,
one ear,
one eye
could be given to others
and one could be
kept for herself.

But,
where only one was made,
must be keep for herself.
One mind,
one heart
and a tongue
to speak both truths.

STARS THAT BURN
the brightest
are those
which are *condensing*.

Becoming quieter,
more potent in yourself
means burning in a silence
that thunders throughout the universe.

A PICTURE

A picture speaks a thousand words. But what can a thousand words portray?

Words do not merely pinch the surface or poke the skin, but grasp the soul by its iridescent chords, untethering it from its source and unraveling it from its cosmic tongue.

Words. Oh words, they have the emotional power of a thousand pictures, of a million moonlit postcards strung by delicate threads off the edge of the universe.

Words are the burning lamps to which all light exists beyond their perceived presence, lingering in the mind like stars on alpine nights.

Words are our inner moons to which we reflect light upon our beloved world and hold space in our silence for the darkness that wishes to turn from the sun.

Words. Oh words, they shape our lives, they motivate our moods into actions and create our physical realities. How simple a sentence like 'I know I can do this' can have on our life's outcome. How simple an emotion like 'love' can have on our ability to be creatively literate.

Words are not pictures, nor do they lower themselves to meet these limiting dimensions. They aspire to the soul as we aspire to find in a mate. To feel the wholeness and resonance that comes from deep connection, to feel the grounding and belonging that come with supportive words. To co-create an extraordinary life with a soul mate is to indeed use the magic blade-bone with written song upon.

We are the sum of our inner dialogues. The stories we tell ourselves. The conversations we surround ourselves with, and the physical words that form in the base of our pallets that sound out into the ethos, reflecting back our inner most desires.

We cannot hide from our words, for they are the transcripts of our lives, the embroidered letters lovingly stitched into the seams of our life. Our path is written by the ink of our emotions and the quill of our desires, setting forth a story of adventure, a tale of love and betrayal, of all that is possible and all that is lost.

We are born sentient...some of us merely linger still in a state of slow slumber, waiting to be lifted, to be roused by a reason to see the world differently. For this is what we wish the most; to tell ourselves a different story to the ones we tell ourselves everyday. The ones that are routinely dumbing us into habit, into conformed rows of little, labeled boxes. These are the stories that have been etched upon our skin's vulnerable husk by the over culture, the undermining few that seek to predict our actions and mute our words of truth.

Instead, we wish to live *another* story, the one we know intuitively, the one that makes us come alive with passion and excitement and feel the ease to which all life becomes a dance with vibration.

I shall tell you these stories, with the words of my inner being, and with the hope that they seep through the veil of time and space, to where we both shall sit and converse with our spirits.

Oh, the words we shall exchange, the oneness we shall melt into. The poetic discourse we shall reel off our heart's typewriter, to which our eloquence shall be envied by the silence of the cosmos.

How beautiful this conversation will be, how connected we shall become, how potently we will be able heal each other, and how inexplicably alive we shall sing ourselves back into our divinity.

Words *are* our discourse divine.

DO NOT USE YOUR PAIN
to validate your loneliness
to excuse your isolation
to justify your fears
to keep you stagnant
in places that
at least
you *know*.

Expand beyond
this limited belief
and if nothing else
know this…

> you are not your pain
> and this pain
> is not yours.

SHE DANCED TO THE UNEASE
of her darkness,
to the shadows beneath her molten core,
to the craters that caved into her heart,
to the bareness of her all.

She danced in the sun's bright warmth
which reflected upon her face,
basked in the light
of the one she loved,
and who adored her Luna ways.

She danced to his ever-gazing affections,
to the distance he allowed her,
to the space she sometimes fell into,
often deeper than she knew it possible to fall.

Ever dancing between their contrasts,
she whispered into the cosmos,
"When I face you, my shadows cast their
emptiness behind me, and I am confronted by the
light which make my eyes burn - But better to be
scorched by light of truth than safe in the cast of
ignorance."

CREATE A LITTLE KINDLE
of self love.

Start small,
like the breathe
that whispers
flame into life.

Learn to shelter it
from the torrid winds
of the outside world
until it becomes
a raging fire
that spreads to all
who dare resonate
with your passion -
and they too,
begin to burn.

Let our world
be seen
from such a great distance,
our foremothers rejoice
in the heavens
and our loved ones

use the light
to find their way home.

Create a little kindle
for self love
and that flame will
become eternal.

TODAY,
I will walk with lightness,
likened to a tiptoe through sand.

I will softly ease myself through the streets,
weave my body among the people,
and sift through places I need to go.

I will let go of these weights in my pocket,
one
by
one
by
one.

Too heavy is the burden of shame,
of doubt, of insecurity.

So today, I choose to let them go.

I let them go, and I walk with lightness,
likened to the nimble heart, which lifts me
in its helium state
to touch the tip
of its weightless liberation.

WE CHASE AWAY DEATH
with battered broomsticks
that we also use
to hide dust under carpets.

We need not deny,
nor hurriedly dismiss
all that makes
our lives unlived
and our houses unkempt.

But air out
all that scares us.

And burn the broom
in rebellious delight.

TRY NOT TO WASTE YOUR TIME
dealing with what you see,
but instead, ask yourself…

"Where
am I
seeing
this
from?"

EGO

Sometimes your ego will dress up as your intuition. She'll dance around, spilling out profound prose about what you need, what will make you most happy and how to get it — because *she* knows you best. *She* loves you more.

She'll run herself ragged and tire herself out trying to convince you of her vital message of 'truth'.

But then... she'll get angry, and her fury will set alight a thousand ideas of self-destruction, her dress tearing to sheds with the need to be seen, to be loved, to be validated.

She'll plead there's no time, that you are wasting your life, how could you not listen to her, what were you waiting for that she could not articulate, that she could not perform in your honor?

Emotion?

She will not understand these words, these vowels that bind you to the inner beat of your true knowing.

She will lay herself down in defeat, but mostly in denial of the fact that she did not win this game.

And in her silence, intuition will whisper to you through a stillness that only befalls upon souls before life and after death – and say,

"Be here, my love. All is coming."

WHAT I FEAR MOST
is the half-dead life.

The neither *this* nor *that* life.

The in-between,
down the crack life.

The one I can't decide
whether I should
or shouldn't life.

Because a limbo life
is a half-dead life
and seems to always be a
lingering in the creases life.

It is a waiting in the sideline life,
a never gets to play life,
because I'm always hesitating
and delaying
and waiting
for the exact right moment
to fully live again life…

ONCE YOU REALIZE
everything
everyone
thinks,
says
and does
is just a reflection
of themselves…

You stop taking things personally.

EVERY MORNING,
we wake
to the two same tools
that shape, mend and restore
our life.

The cookie-cutter
or
the handmade blade.

Which one will you use today?

I DO NOT WANT
to swim upstream
against the masses
of numbed-out minds.

I want to pull myself up
out of the water
and onto the land,
sprouting legs,
muscle,
bone
and ligaments,
and walk certain-footed
upon solid land.

I no longer want to be part
of primal scales,
of gills and fins,
of bulging eyes,
of consensus and conformity.

I want to be the end state
of millenniums,
of expansion and adaptation,
of trial and error.

A mutant
of nature's conscious laboratory.

I Want To Evolve.

FOLLOW YOUR LOVE

Follow your love, veraciously. Yield to it over and over again. Even if you have been wounded. *Especially* when you have been wounded, for it is the only healing power with the purpose of regeneration.

Shake your roots and see what you have already prepared. Notice years and years worth of love's fallen residue, the ashes from loss, the basaltic soil from depressions – see the blackened volcanic nutrition that has formed by your feet, preparing you for your most magnificent bloom yet.

Although your heartache is profound, you are not standing in the baron planes of a soul-famine. No, not if you save some of your tears to moisture the ground of which you will grow stronger upon.

Nurture your love in truth, for to demand it again out of anger, in hate or in loneliness is not to know love at all.

LIVE LIFE FLESHED OUT,
kneaded out of bone and breathe,
of salted sweat
and the sweetness of love.

Touch life's substance,
its un-shallowable marrow,
it's pith and fiber
that sustains the starved Spirit.

HOW DO I KNOW

*M*e: *How do I know if what I am doing is right?*

Universe: You are creating a reaction. You are creating a community. You are creating friction. You are creating a tribe. You are creating people who fear, who love, who embrace, who push back. Most importantly you are creating a response to what you are doing.

You should only ever worry when people are indifferent towards you.

I AM NOT MADE OF RICE PAPER,
or Anemone blade.

I am not made of threadbare silk
or the tapered edges
of old colony glass.

I cannot split or tear
at my many-folded edges
or fray at the heels
of my well trodden feet.

I will not snap
from bitter word
or be chewed up
by soured tongues.

I am made of bone and blood,
of cartilage and course skin,
and this shall not break me.

No, this shall just remind me
of my substance.

HOW DOES YOUR BODY
move,
lift,
bend,
embrace,
dance,
feel...

It doesn't matter
what size
what shape
what ratio of flesh to bone
there is...

A healing body
is an expressive body.

I FEAR NO DARKNESS,
no shadow,
no umbra.

I revel in its contrast,
its luminous veil
that allows me to rest
and find retreat
in the enfolds of obscurity.

I am a child of the shadows,
a lover of the cracks
to which all manner
of depth
anchors me in an expanse,
of art and expression,
of passion and creation.

I am master of my darkness
like the goddess, Nyx.
Mother of shadows.
Maiden of raven wings. The one
who's ebony body
births the stars at dusk…

I fear no darkness
because she is my creator.

ALTHOUGH THOSE HARD WORDS
might dismantle you
entirely,

Remember the *one*
that came from kindness…

and resurrect yourself from that.

FLUSHED

Flushed by the kiss of frost, I boldly tread upon the newly fallen snow. The bone chilling, Nordic air slips into the gapes of my threadbare socks and invites the chill in. Crunch and bite under foot echoes through the thin air, breaking ghostly breezes that flicker life into the baron hawthorn bush. This - the dead of winter - the solstice of Yule, these blackened days so tightly strung they march my heart to its rhythmic melancholy.

I walk to blend myself into the monochrome, to allow myself to dim into the backdrop, to give myself permission to feel the bereft of Sun's warmth. For, although this winter is my kin, one that welcomes me back again into her stone hearth, I have forgotten its house-rules and more importantly its burdening inheritance.

I walk until the ice begins to churn beneath the bare ash tree, its branches tilting in agreement with the wind, and kneel beside the bee house in solitary setting - to which I expect to be met with a silent abode.

I have not come here since high summer, where the bees danced in chaotic synchronicity on the breath of life to which all rejoiced. What shall I find here, I utter in unspoken words, if nothing but the beggared and deprived shells of what once was alive with purpose and hustle. My ear presses into the box's frosty surface with hope for still life in the hive.

From deep within its burrowed heart, the faint flutters of small wings tap melodically, feeding the Queen her warmth, still in service but now in confinement to the winter's dormant veil. Their hums pattern the tapestry of life with instinctual knowledge; to resonate, to vibrate, to survive. My heart falls into rhythm with their tune and rhapsodizes, *still life in these little woods, still life in these hives.*

Renewed, I walk towards the blackberry bush, a shield maiden in arms, with its thorns and razor-cut leaves tired from a season of defense. The robin sits among its armory, a stark contrast in daintiness and color. Her breast proudly heaving in the cold air, her little black elderberry eyes scanning the bush for remnants of lasts years pickings. You see, there is still life in these little woods, she beams, *still softness in this place of defense.*

Shards of green grass cut between sheets of ice, the snow peas, and the crocus still unfurl in the frightful cold. These early bloomers, these late blossom-ers, untimely in their showmanship, but flourishing when there is most need of distinction, not when there is an a agreement in conditions. The holly tree, the ever greens, the fickle fern and the pine, all contrast their mossy tones against the earth's bare pastels.

I too, shall not fade into the background like so many times before, but grow thorns and waxed leaves to endure the slow season of change. I too shall nestle my softness among the harsh furrows of snow and ice, and sing gently into the silent winds.

I need not feel nostalgia for days past, nor long for the warmer ones to come, but learn to grow slower, to blossom later, to peek through the hardships and contrast with burning chest, crimson berry and prickled edge to get through the winter with introspection and resolution. For I shall not grow evanescent or ephemeral like the tulip and the poppy. I will not lie dormant, waiting for life to nourish me, but take what is here and now, and show brave contrast against the desolation.

That is my winter's purpose - to vibrate within my own inner cluster, to look after the monarch within who needs a season of regeneration and renewal. To take the ravaged bushes of life and make a protective inner-home, to peek through the cold with just a hint of color and to feel that slow, silent and deep inwardness - that slow-brewed transformation - that brings such potency.

❖

Be not like the fragile flowers, I ask of you, who blossom in the perfect but fleeting conditions of high summer - but like the small life that reverberates silently in the dead of winter, in the relentless darkness. Find your moment with winter's moon, your resonance with Luna who will birth the sun once again in the midst of her own solstice. Be the contrast in the still air, the sweet song on the dry wind. For there is life in these small woods, there is life among the wilted and waiting that renews and restores.

REMEMBER PRECIOUS STONES
in pockets
and pine cones
in shoes.

Remember sand filled cuffs
and straight sticks
that poked holes
and flicked acorns.

The keeper of special things
and daydreams.

The walker
among hydrangeas,
barefooted but tough soled.

She still lives,
the hide and seeker,
in those who dare
hold on
to all that
which still line pockets,
not with daisies and dirt,
but hope and resilience.

TRAVEL LIGHTLY.

Leave little pieces
of your soul
in the salted spirals
of the nautilus,
under oriental moons,
with barefooted children
and in the palms
of those
more wise
and more weathered.

Return heavy,
from the weight of awe.

THE WOMAN WHO KEEPS HERSELF -
who saves a piece of herself -
retains the energy,
the light
and the love
for not only herself
but for others too.

The woman who holds space for herself,
who chooses herself,
who allows herself
time
is not a perfect sister, partner, mother…
but a magnificent woman.

The woman who lives in freedom,
in passion,
in soul-fulfilling creation,
who muses on the heaviness
of the over culture
and floats with a lightness
and ease
through the drudge
of expectation
and judgment…

She is not only immaculate woman
but Mother to Spirit,
Child to Earth,
Sister to Circles.
And incarnation
of the Sombra Soul.

To be mother of life,
is to be woman first.

To be balanced
is not to adjust the scales,
but to swing the pendulum
back into place -
letting it fall into equilibrium
from the density of self-love.

I HAVE COME TO SEE
the value of silencing the crowds,
of walking away,
and of muting the false cheers
that celebrate the mundane.

I have come to see
the value of listening to myself,
and have ambitioned
to only ever please
this audience of one,
my sold out inner theatre -
and its only attendee.

For when she celebrates
me through my authenticity,
I vibrate into a thousand
strands of spun-silk
into the liquid sun.

YOU KNOW WHAT FEELS RIGHT,
what lifts your soul,
what nourishes your being,
what sets your pulse alight.

You *know* how it feels
to be completely filled
within the glove
that is your unique self,
to reach into every stitch
of who *you* are.

Let those who live limply
be in their own incompleteness,
and live - love - laugh
into what makes you unconditionally **full**.

WHAT ARE THESE THREADS

What are these threads, but spun yarn to cover the imperfections of my excellence? You made me believe I am not worthy to be seen by the naked eye of truth but to be constrained within the tightly woven cloth of my false beliefs. No cloth shall be made in my honor, I shall craft no thread but bare my skin to elements of likeness in Earth, Air, Fire and Water. I shall leave you on the shore, your dishonest dyes to be faded by the sun's unrelenting authenticity. *I shall be free of you, and I shall return to my tide.*

What are these shoes, but the stepping stones of history treading the same footprints over and over again, impeding on the sand a heavy foot of habit. You do not serve me, and have made me walk so long without direction that I no longer know from where I came from. My soles are swollen from the ingrained marks upon which your hard leather has coursed into my feet. I want to create a new footprint, a new pattern that has no trademark but is washed by the foam of every breaking day, to start anew. I shall leave you here, laced and polished for the gratitude in your shaping of me but for the crabs to dismember you with their own persistent hunger for what has been and cannot be changed.

I shall be free of you, and I shall return to my tide.

What are these jewels that dress my body in service to the future. Merely decorations of promise, of hope to be grasped for greedy embellishment. I want not ambition of this kind, I hold no desire for the poison that seeps from their sparkle into my blood that burns me to want more. I have more than most, and that is to always have *enough*. I shall leave you here, to catch the evening light's reflection so that you may create a mirage for the birds to tenaciously circle. With compassion for the dreams you unraveled me with, I let you go but let this isolation teach you of my mortality because my future is of my own craftsmanship and I have no illusion of your collaborative promises.

I shall be free of you, and I shall return to my tide.

What of now, I ask, what of my bones now bared unto the ocean's tide. I offer what is left of me, what is *now*, unto its soft folds of foam and matter. This liquidity of life, of ebb and flow, of deepness and ripple. I shall return to this state of true nature, enveloped into its uncertainty, but without fear. The lapping coolness, soothing my fiery soul with her inexplicable sense of belonging. My tide holds the current of life that yields in its suppleness reflections of the moon, and she too, rides with me. Of crescent and crest we dance in the surf. A melody of freedom and union, of swells and spindrifts.

- Past, Future & Present

THE FABRIC OF ME
is Mother,
the weft and warp,
Woman.

Loosely woven,
I am free.

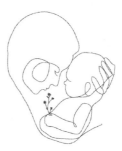

ONE DAY,
at the end of your long journey,
you will realize that everything
you have been searching for
was not to be found –
but to be **created**.

SOMETIMES, TO HEAL A WOUND
is to learn how to simply live *with* it.

For, like an impaired eye
heightens other senses,
so will this wound
strengthen your soul-sense.

WHEN DID WE FORGET
our gratitude for subtlety?
How did we come
to easily overlook the details?

Perhaps it was when
we decided seasons should be 4
and not the subtle nuances
of 365 individual days,
each dynamic
with 365 stages of life.

Or perhaps it was in hurriedness
in making the 12 hour clock
that we left out the exquisitely long night
that makes for 24 full hours.

Or perhaps it was when
we thought healing was a prescription
and not a process,
or when rest was a nap
and not a hibernation.

When did we forget
the richness and potency

of a slow brewed life,
the simple and subtlety
of a dynamic and compelling life?

Perhaps if we learnt
that for change to occur
we needed to notice
the incremental moments
that make a whole life,
and not just expect change itself.

Imagine catching the first trace of salt
in the air
before the liquid horizon meets you.

Or sensing the first sign of
imbalance in your body
before disease seizes.

Touching the first tight bud
in late winter
before the blossoms of Spring…

These are the small gaps
where magic falls

into a world of unseen subtlety.

Be subtle, *know* subtle, *feel* subtle
and never miss the life
that moves beneath your feet.

CUT A WOMAN FROM HER ROOTS,
her soul-driven life,
is like taking a sprig
from the blossoming cherry tree
and displaying it in a vase
with the hope that it too
may flourish magnificently.

SALT ENCRUSTED HAIR STRANDS,
pumpkin shells
and lightning whelks.

Warm gusts
from the Indian swell
and half buried
red sand verbena.

Sliding dunes
and pineapple juice,
pigeon coo and gull squawk.
The prickle of dried grass
and passion fruit pips
under foot…

Let what takes you home
take you inward
and not to the places
of longing,
but to the familiarity of *knowing*.

KNOW THE DIFFERENCE
between *allowing* and *procrastination* intimately.

One feels
like you are
yet
to know
exactly
what you
need
to know
in order to
move forward
in faith and certainty.

The others feels
like you already know
what you need to do -
but fear
the change
too much.

YOUR LITTLE HEART
once beat through mine.
And unlike the
synchronized footsteps
that break weakened bridges,
yours strengthened mine.

And I likened myself
to a woman of resolution,
bound to a responsibility
of self nourishment.

For if I were to live a day
in the empty shell of care,
so too would you
become bereft of your home.

And if I were to forge
my ideals upon you, unwillingly,
so too would you be
victimized by your inheritance.

And if I were to sacrifice my own life
to live through yours,
so too would you become

but shuck and sheath to
the vibrant bloom of your own making.

Your little heart
once beat through mine
and rebirthed a woman
who suddenly prayed
for her own life.

- Self-care and motherhood

CHOOSE NOT TO BE
the short-blooming poppy
that burgeons in high summer
under cloudless skies
and long, warm days.

But the thistle, whose violet head peaks
in the dead of winter
to feed the remaining bees
with its honey suckled pins
and ever green bristles.

WHAT IS LIFE

What *is* *life* but the opportunity to experience everything and leave nothing but the remnants of goodness in those who carry on. *What of our purpose,* but to touch the souls of everyone we are fortunate enough to love. *What of our individuality,* if not to live according to our own blueprints. *What of our love,* if not to empower ourselves with the ability to see beyond reason. *What of our pain,* if not to learn how to embrace transformation. *What of our darkness,* if not to notice contrast and shades that create masterpieces. *What of our suffering,* if not to allow us the chance to transcend all illusions. *What of our future,* if not to be intended by our own hands. *What of consciousness,* if not to give ourselves the sacred right to be truly present to our life. *And what of the sacred feminine psyche,* if not to liberate us into the alignment of self-healing.

For without HER, we have no means of nurture, no compassion, no empowerment that comes from allowing spaces between divine connection.

What is life, but the consistent opportunity to find our way back to HER again?

YOU ARE NOT ALONE, BRAVE SOUL.
You are more aligned
with yourself
and that causes others to fear.

Find those
who keep the golden feather
stitched into their pockets
and who speak with
consciousness to their life.

They are your tribe
and you will be among those rare beings
who see with an immaculate heart.

You are not alone, brave soul.
You are just living in contrast,
not in truth.

HERE LIES WOMAN,
both willow tree and palm,
both crest and belly
to ocean,
both canopy and undergrowth
to forest,
and at the same time -
nothing to the elements
but a soft hurricane.

Dear honored reader,

I am a South African born, bohemian-soul – now living in the Nordic wilderness with a Danish husband and a little tribe of Viking tots. I write about self-healing, awakening and thriving through emotional darkness. I would love to connect, empower and support you on your own journey – together; we are able to live deeper, with more authenticity, meaning and connected to the profound guidance of Spirit.

Please feel free to stay in touch beyond the book via:
https://www.sezkristiansen.com/
@sezkristiansen

If you felt this book would be of help to others, please **review it on Amazon** so that it may be seen by more potential readers, and I sincerely thank you for your time!

With Gratitude,
Sez

Made in the USA
Middletown, DE
08 August 2020